Dear Reader,

As you begin your journey through this devotional, I pray each page will serve to draw you closer to Jesus. Over the next 30 days, you are invited to take a few moments each day reflecting on His immense love for you.

Each Scripture reference is designed for you to look up in your Bible and then write it out in this book. This will help you to hide God's Word in your own heart and fill your mind with His sweet promises for you.

Let's keep taking every step with Jesus as we are daily abiding in His Word and keeping our eyes fixed on Him.

In Christ,
Marquita
Romans 8:28

Day 1

Bible Verse For Today
Psalm 25:5
Look Up The Verse(s) and Write Out Below

_____

_____

_____

_____

Devotional Thought

May this be the prayer of our hearts today and always.
God's truth is precious beyond words.
Truly knowing Him is the source of our all hope.

Day 2

Bible Verse For Today

Philippians 4:19

Look Up The Verse(s) and Write Out Below

___

___

___

___

Devotional Thought

We are blessed to have a personal relationship with the Creator of the universe. To know He calls each of us personally by name. Rest in today's promise. He knows our needs better than we do ourselves. Let's humbly surrender to Him and He will show us His ways.

Day 3

Bible Verse For Today
Psalm 100:1-2
Look Up The Verse(s) and Write Out Below

_____

_____

_____

_____

♥♥♥

Devotional Thought

This is the day God has made and we get to rejoice in Him EVERY single minute of it. Fill the hours with singing praise songs to Jesus! Take time to reflect on the ways He has provided for you through the years. An attitude of gratitude really does make a difference.

Day 4

Bible Verse For Today

2 Timothy 1:7

Look Up The Verse(s) and Write Out Below

Devotional Thought

Let us turn our minds and hearts towards Jesus all the day long. Our foe may try to pull us down with fear, but Jesus has said No. He has not given us a spirit of fear but rather a spirit of power, love, and a sound mind. Let's CHOOSE to listen to Jesus every moment.

Day 5

Bible Verse For Today

John 10:27-28

Look Up The Verse(s) and Write Out Below

_____

_____

_____

_____

♥♥♥

Devotional Thought

Our Shepherd is calling all of us to follow Him today. There may be other voices out in the world telling us to go a different way, to follow the more popular path. But the voice of Jesus is the only one that is truly safe to lead us all the way home.

Day 6

Bible Verse For Today
Revelation 3:20
Look Up The Verse(s) and Write Out Below

_____

_____

_____

_____

♥♥♥

Devotional Thought

Welcome to a new day with Jesus! And what a precious thought~the One who died for us also walks with us. Jesus desires to have a personal relationship with each one of us that lasts a lifetime~an ETERNAL lifetime! Do you hear Him knocking on the door of your heart right now? Invite Him in.

Day 7

Bible Verse For Today
Psalm 62:1-2
Look Up The Verse(s) and Write Out Below

_____

_____

_____

_____

♥♥♥

Devotional Thought

True rest is found in God. Our daily experience with Him enables us to forge through whatever circumstances may come our way. So for today, whether we find ourselves high on the mountaintop or down low in the valley, God is there. In the heart of each moment, our souls can choose to find strength and rest in His abiding presence.

Day 8

Bible Verse For Today
Psalm 118:1
Look Up The Verse(s) and Write Out Below

_____

_____

_____

_____

♥♥♥

Devotional Thought

Today we get to choose to look up into the heavens and KNOW where our help comes from~Jesus. His mercy is everlasting even during the hard times. Let's ask Him today to show us His ways for our lives. Let's surrender everything to Him and see what He does.

Day 9

Bible Verse For Today
Revelation 1:8
Look Up The Verse(s) and Write Out Below

___

___

___

___

♥♥♥

Devotional Thought

May Jesus open our eyes to see Him for who He really is today. We know the enemy roars like a lion seeking to devour us, BUT Jesus has said He is the great "I AM". May we truly understand the majesty and power of the magnificent God we worship and adore.

Day 10

Bible Verse For Today

John 16:33

Look Up The Verse(s) and Write Out Below

___

Devotional Thought

Let's take time today to really hide this verse in our hearts. God's Word is strength to our minds and bodies. It is our privilege to "digest" as much of His Word as we can, for we do not know what tomorrow brings. Days are coming when our Bibles may not be available to us, but the Word that is in us can never be taken away.

Day 11

Bible Verse For Today

Isaiah 26:3

Look Up The Verse(s) and Write Out Below

Devotional Thought

The Lord is our Help during every moment of the day. The world is growing shakier with each passing day, but Jesus is our Rock, our firm foundation in the midst of all shifting sand. Let's choose His Peace today.

Day 12

Bible Verse For Today

Acts 4:12

Look Up The Verse(s) and Write Out Below

_____

_____

_____

_____

Devotional Thought

Priorities in our lives are shifting. God in His mercy is giving us time right now to be strengthened. He is our salvation and it is imperative we cultivate a lifestyle today that enables us to distinguish His voice from other voices. He alone is our Safety.

Day 13

Bible Verse For Today
Galatians 6:9
Look Up The Verse(s) and Write Out Below

_____

_____

_____

_____

Devotional Thought

Today the Lord will give us opportunities to love Him by loving others. The world may be growing dark and cold, but the truth of Jesus still shines brightly and creates warmth in the heart. Let's show the world around us that He makes all the difference!

Day 14

Bible Verse For Today
Exodus 14:13-14
Look Up The Verse(s) and Write Out Below

_____

_____

_____

_____

Devotional Thought

It is so easy for us to trust in ourselves for solutions, isn't it? But God says when we take the time ~ TIME ~ to be still in His presence ~ to repent, surrender, and become humble ~ He will SHOW us how He is fighting for us. Let's take time today to BE STILL in His Word and see what Jesus does right in front of us.

Day 15

Bible Verse For Today
Lamentations 3:22-23
Look Up The Verse(s) and Write Out Below

_____

_____

_____

_____

♥♥♥

Devotional Thought

God's Word is truly nourishment for our souls. We can trust Jesus to be faithful through ALL circumstances. We get to choose to focus on Him through the storm. Let's feast on His goodness and mercy. His Spirit will empower us to love the unlovely and be the salt of the earth. Why? So others may taste and see the Lord is indeed good.

Day 16

Bible Verse For Today
Psalm 121:2
Look Up The Verse(s) and Write Out Below

_____

_____

_____

_____

Devotional Thought

What a wonderful God we serve! All throughout creation we see evidences of His deep love for us. From the highest mountain to the lowest valley, from the deepest ocean to the widest desert, He is inviting us to recognize Him as Creator of all. May His Spirit show us that He alone is our true Help in every situation.

Day 17

Bible Verse For Today
Psalm 139:23-24

Look Up The Verse(s) and Write Out Below

_____

_____

_____

♥♥♥

Devotional Thought

Do we have the courage to ask the Holy Spirit to do some "heart" cleansing? By God's grace, let's become even more careful about the things we say, the words we write, and how we conduct our daily lives. Let's make the most of every moment He gives us to let His kindness, goodness, and mercy shine through us to others.

Day 18

Bible Verse For Today
Psalm 91:2
Look Up The Verse(s) and Write Out Below

_____

_____

_____

_____

Devotional Thought

What can we say about our Lord today? Troubles may be mounting all around, but He has prepared a place of safety for those who trust in Him. Let's pray today for our hearts to be opened to His Majesty and how much He truly loves us.

Day 19

Bible Verse For Today

Psalm 147:4

Look Up The Verse(s) and Write Out Below

_____

_____

_____

_____

♥♥♥

Devotional Thought

As we drove home, my daughter exclaimed, "Mom! Look at the stars!" It was a clear night and as far as the eye could see, twinkling stars adorned the sky. Our Father has so many ways to lovingly remind us of His great care. For if He cares enough to call even the stars by name, how much more does He care for you?

Day 20

Bible Verse For Today
James 4:10
Look Up The Verse(s) and Write Out Below

_____

_____

_____

_____

♥♥♥

Devotional Thought

Our emotions can be stretched to the limit by those who seek to bring us down. But let us remember ~ when we allow the Holy Spirit to do His work of humility in our hearts today, He will be the One to lift us up during the trials of tomorrow.

Day 21

Bible Verse For Today
Psalm 29:11
Look Up The Verse(s) and Write Out Below

___

♥♥♥

Devotional Thought

Remember the song, Jesus Loves Me? There's a line that says, "They are weak, but He is strong." On days when we may feel we are at the end of our rope, Jesus is right there. His strength is made perfect in our weakness. Trust in His great love for you today.

Day 22

Bible Verse For Today

Isaiah 41:13

Look Up The Verse(s) and Write Out Below

_____

_____

_____

_____

Devotional Thought

Have you ever imagined holding the hand of God Himself? As we go through life, there will be times we feel as though we are stumbling, just like a little child learning to walk. But just as a loving parent holds onto that little one, God is holding us every step of the way. Keep looking up and reaching for His strong yet gentle hand.

Day 23

Bible Verse For Today

Psalm 42:8

Look Up The Verse(s) and Write Out Below

_____

_____

_____

_____

♥♥♥

Devotional Thought

The Lord desires for us to know His presence is with us at all times, even while we sleep. Many times I have awakened during the night to have a Bible promise come to mind. God's promises are like songs. They bring us comfort and peace. Be strong in the Lord ~ day and night.

Day 24

Bible Verse For Today
Psalm 48:14
Look Up The Verse(s) and Write Out Below

_____

_____

_____

_____

Devotional Thought

Every day is filled with decisions. Sometimes we may struggle with which way to go. In these moments, God invites us to stop and reach for His Word. All we need do is look for Him and follow what He shows us. The answer is not much in looking for the solution itself as it is focusing on Him ~ the Solution-Maker.

Day 25

Bible Verse For Today

John 10:10

Look Up The Verse(s) and Write Out Below

___

___

___

___

♥♥♥

Devotional Thought

As followers of Christ, we are in the midst of a ferocious battle. The enemy seeks to steal, kill, and destroy us. He is cunning enough to make something sound good that is actually to our detriment. Remember Eve at the tree? BUT Jesus has said we may have LIFE through Him ~ and more abundantly. Let's choose God's way.

Day 26

Bible Verse For Today

John 4:23-24

Look Up The Verse(s) and Write Out Below

_____

_____

_____

_____

♥♥♥

Devotional Thought

Jesus meets with the woman at the well. Her life is a wreck. But Jesus walks into her life at the moment of her greatest need. He knew her heart. He invited her to be a true worshiper of our Father in heaven. Jesus knows our hearts too. The good, the bad, the ugly. Everything. And yet, He loves us and invites us to find new life in Him.

Day 27

Bible Verse For Today
Genesis 50:21
Look Up The Verse(s) and Write Out Below

___

Devotional Thought

As with Joseph, God is working in our lives in ways we cannot see. Joseph experienced years of pain and disappointment. Yet, God was weaving a master plan that unfolded in results surpassing Joseph's wildest dreams. Trust God to turn your trials into triumphs at just the right time. Accept His gift to live by faith and not by sight.

Day 28

Bible Verse For Today
I Chronicles 29:11
Look Up The Verse(s) and Write Out Below

_____

_____

_____

_____

Devotional Thought

Are there words adequate enough to describe our God? We have the privilege to rest in His Presence and let Him renew our minds and refresh our hearts. Reflect on the ways He has led in your life, especially during the hard times. When we recall what He has done in the past, our faith will grow for what He will do in the future.

Day 29

Bible Verse For Today
Psalm 1:1-3
Look Up The Verse(s) and Write Out Below

_____

_____

_____

_____

♥♥♥

Devotional Thought

Psalm 1 is filled with tremendous counsel and hope for our day. Take time to read the whole chapter. There is a blessing waiting for us when we heed the words of our loving Heavenly Father.

Day 30

Bible Verse For Today
Psalm 93:1
Look Up The Verse(s) and Write Out Below

_____

_____

_____

_____

♥♥♥

Devotional Thought

Take time to go outside today and look at the bigger picture of all that is around you. Gaze up to the sky and see how expansive the heavens are from east to west. Soak in all the beauty of creation as you listen for the breeze and breathe in the fresh air. The One who watches even the little sparrow has His loving eye upon you.

For More Devotional Resources
www.MomentsWithJesus.org